Chapter & Illuminating Verse

*Helping to Throw Light
on Parkinson's Disease*

By
Becky Hurd and Ray Wegrzyn

With images by
Ghislaine Howard

Published by Ray Wegrzyn, 2011

Set in 10/12pt Minion. Designed, typeset and printed by Cygnus Printing, Glossop.

ISBN: 978-0-9569887-0-6

Contents

Foreword

To introduce this book of poems really is quite humbling
Aware that rhyming with said word could lead to so much stumbling
Over words and phrases put together to enable us to say
How much we'd like to thank our friend Becky and her mate Ray
For giving us the opportunity to be a part
Of something filled with fantastic verse and amazing works of art
Becky and Ray have truly painted a picture of how it is to be
A young person living with a disease of the elderly
Or so we thought until Becky told us of her plight
And with her we stand as a united front and together we must fight
This book will help raise much needed funds to help to find a cure
So please give generously to them and generate some more
The funds will hopefully help all those people who are living with PD
So Becky & Ray, good luck with your book, from Chapter Agency

Acknowledgements

Our thanks go to:

Our families – for everything;

Ghislaine Howard for her willingness to support us, her tolerance, and her beautiful artwork;

Jodi Cook for his generosity of time and his skill at layout;

Everyone who proofread or commented. You're too many to name but you know who you are.

Becky Hurd

Becky Hurd was diagnosed with Young Onset Parkinson's Disease in August 2005 aged just 29.

Three years later in 2008, Becky decided she wanted to help raise awareness of the condition, based on her experience of people's lack of understanding, and ultimately to fundraise.

Becky set herself a goal to raise £100,000 for Parkinson's research. Using her professional experience in marketing and PR, she started working with Trevor Owen to create the beginnings of a committee. Shortly after meeting Trevor, Becky rejoined forces with ex-colleagues from Chapter, a marketing agency in the West Midlands.

Becky formally founded Illuminate in October 2008, a brand developed by Ian, Martin and Mike, the three partners from Chapter. Illuminate was to become the brand to front all of her fundraising efforts which involved funding research to find a cure for Parkinson's as well as supporting those people living with the condition to enjoy a full and enriched life.

Becky's first fundraising event was the Illuminate Ball in April 2010, a spectacular black-tie ball which raised £30,000.

On a professional level, as her condition has deteriorated, Becky has been finding new ways to enable her to continue to work for as long as her condition will allow. This has included setting up her marketing consultancy business – Lumatime Ltd.

Becky is married to John and has a daughter, Mollie. Family life is Becky's main motivation, both hers and others who fight this dreadful condition. She addresses this by maintaining her commitment to raise funds to help fight Parkinson's on many different fronts.

Ray Wegrzyn

Ray Wegrzyn lives in Glossop, Derbyshire. He was one of Her Majesty's Inspectors of Probation until he had to retire due to ill health in June 2011. Prior to taking up that role in 2002, he served his career as a probation officer in the Greater Manchester Probation Service working mainly in Salford and Oldham. In 1995 Ray was diagnosed with Young Onset Parkinson's Disease at the age of 39. He considers himself to have been fortunate with the slow development of his condition and he continued to work full-time until July 2010.  In more recent years, however, as the condition has begun to limit him, he has started to focus his energies on doing something for others facing similar challenges.

Ray joined with Becky Hurd in writing this collection in part as a way of venting some of his frustration with his increasing disability. Ray is keen to highlight the impact Parkinson's can have beyond the visible symptoms. He said, "This condition can be devastating in terms of intellectual and emotional functioning as much as any physical disability it produces. That being said, people with Parkinson's can continue to make a full contribution to society, even if they may need a little support to do so.

"*Chapter and Illuminating Verse* is an edgy read. It is not meant to comfort anyone. Nor is it intended to suggest that everyone with Parkinson's will feel the same emotions described within. The dark humour expressed demonstrates that anything life can throw, whatever the immediate impact, can also be laughed at. If people find the poetry not to their taste, then Ghislaine's art provides a feast of visual joy. We are so grateful for her support.

"We have also ended the collection very deliberately with a section that is about hope. There is so much work going on in many different fields of research and we know that huge efforts are being made to find a cure. Yes, it's a long slow process, but ultimately we do think that there will be a solution to this condition and we very much look forward to it being something that we can benefit from."

Ghislaine Howard

Ghislaine Howard lives and works in Glossop in the North West of England. She was named a Woman of the Year in 2008 for her contribution to art and society.

Her motivation is to record and interpret through her work our shared journey from conception to death, to celebrate what Paul Klee called "the dark joy of living." Her ground-breaking exhibition at Manchester Art Gallery, *A Shared Experience*, concerning pregnancy and birth, was the first of its kind.

Her large cycle of paintings *The Stations of the Cross/The Captive Figure*, created in association with Amnesty International, tours cathedrals around the UK. In 2009 Imperial War Museum North exhibited her *365 Series*, a selection from the paintings she makes on a daily basis in response to news media imagery.

In 2011 Ghislaine worked with Salford University's Podiatry Department to produce a body of work entitled The Choreography of Walking and she is currently working with York Minster on an exciting three year project that will culminate in 2013.

Ghislaine exhibits in her own studio gallery in Glossop (www.ghislainehoward.com), with the Cynthia Corbett Gallery in London, and Wendy J Levy Contemporary Art Manchester. She has featured in various publications and television documentaries and her work is represented in many public and private collections including the Royal collection.

Ghislaine's mother, Maureen, suffers from Parkinson's disease and features in many of her works.

List of images by Ghislaine Howard

Chapter 1

Diagnosis

What would it be?

So there I was, what would it be?
I sat there still in the surgery
but you are far too young you see
You have this thing, its called PD

I want you to see another man
To get a second opinion if you can
This wasn't in my life's plan
To go and have a DAT scan

So this is me, take or leave
For my former life I do grieve
PD at 29, who'd believe
Not me, for I was naïve

That fateful day so soon it came
There was no one, nothing to blame
Like others, I wanted to be the same
I didn't want fortune or fame

But fame it was to be mine
I was diagnosed aged just 29
What was this, some holy sign
That I should learn to toe the line?

But time has passed and pills I take
To combat symptoms PD makes
This demonic spell I'd like to break
To stop this inner earthquake

How Many Neuros?

How many neuros does it take
To confirm that you have a shake
To confirm that something's definitely not right
To confirm that its not your ears or sight

How many neuros will say to you
Without much further ado
It's Parkinson's Disease that you have got
It's Parkinson's Disease and that's your lot

How many neuros do you see
One in Brum for my PD
One neuro is all you need
To manage this dreadful disease

Who Gave You The Right?

Who gave you the right
To give this thing a name
I'd been going round for a while
With no name to blame

But on that very fateful day
You had to pipe up and tell me
That what was making me shake
Was called Parkinson's, known as PD

So PD it was known as
From this very point on
And so finally the ambiguity
That was here, has now gone

Mother and Child, oil on canvas, 1985

How Do They Diagnose
The Undiagnosable?

So how do they diagnose the undiagnosable?
It's said there is no definitive test
To misdiagnose would be irresponsible
So I guess they do their level best

X-rays, scans and tests galore
Ruling things out time and again
Until as for tests… there are no more
And they give you their final decision

Parkinson's Disease is what they believe
But diagnosing the young is done seldomly
For my future I now grieve
As isn't this a disease of the elderly?

Child Climbing Stairs, oil on canvas, 1985

Diagnosis

In limbo-like state, I sit and I wait,
for word from a man I don't know and can't hate.
He's going to condemn me for the rest of my life,
a sentence passed, when I have caused no strife,
not committed a crime, nor assaulted my wife.

Look me right in the eye, and I'll tell you why
I believe I should not be given this lot.
It's because, well, it's not fair, it's not as if I wasn't there
to take my fair share, to show that I care.

Wait, there's more, I think… I'm flustered, do you hear
wish I had a drink, it might numb the fear
I'm feeling as I sit and I wait in limbo-like state
for word from a man…

Ageism

"You're far too young," he said to me
muttering under his breath
"It's Parkinson's but I just don't see
how it can be, I'll have to check"

I just want my life back
I don't want to be on this rack
and if I could I would give all the fame back
just to hold my daughter alone

Words

Parkinson's: an affliction.
But so much more.
A deviation from my planned life
a new direction, riddled with strife.

Degenerative: it gets worse.
There is a lesson to be learnt
and until then you get your fingers burnt
lots of little losses – get used to it.

Neurotransmitter: tech speak.
and it takes time to realise
that it's all about a you
that you don't recognise

Dopamine: a neurochemical
or as my wife calls it:
"dope of mine"
that's a me I don't recognise (and she loves me really)

Life: a journey
we all travel it
and we're all the same in as much as
we're all different.

Chapter 2

Carry On
As Normal

Turn Back the Clock

When I was young I had lots of fun
I'd run round playing the fool
At 11 years old I was learning lots
at my new high school

At 16 I went to Gordonstoun
For a scholarship interview
At 18 I went to Lancaster
Being away was really new

At 19 I was in the States
At 20, in Mexico
At 21, back in Lancaster
It really was all go

But 21 was when it happened,
the thing that changed my life
For a compound break of the wrist
has given me trauma and strife

For I believe it was the shock
Of the fracture to my wrist
That sent shockwaves into my brain
Making the chemicals resist

At 29 it became clear
That something was not the same
It took a neurologist or two
To say it was my brain

The diagnosis of PD
Really was a shock
It was at that point in time
I wanted to turn back the clock

Right back to the early days
When I'd play and have fun
But I know that is not possible
My younger days are gone

Be Still

Be still, oh please be still
Please, don't put me on show
I try, I try with all my will
To stop when you say go
And yet, when I choose to move
The big freeze? For Heaven's sake
Oh why do you so disapprove?
Of the choices that I make
It's like you're trying to stake your claim
Trying to take over my life
To bend and twist, to pinch and maim
Subjecting anguish and strife
I've let you in for far too long
There's room in here just for me
I'm sorry, friend, you don't belong
Be gone! Mr. PD!

Sleep

Oh how I wish that I could sleep
A wonderful sleep, oh so deep
The kind that refreshes your body and soul
Making you feel together, whole.
Sleep for me would be a gift from the Gods
A thought with which I am currently at odds
I try time and again to go to bed
To fall asleep and catch some zzzzzzzzz's

Mother and Child Walking, acrylic and charcoal on panel, 2009

I Like Driving in my Car

I'd just been told, but then the choice
Do I tell work? do I use my voice?
To let them know that I have PD
What would that mean for me?

I'd once heard that you don't have to say
If there is anything wrong, you know, in that way
But I felt I needed to say a word
Because it wouldn't take long for that little bird

You see, I'd been struggling with lids and stuff
And with clutch pedals I'd simply had enough
I'd blown up two gearboxes in my car
And to be honest I'd not travelled that far

For it was my left leg sticking on the clutch
That was causing the company car "problem" and as such
The reaction I had was pretty great
They just ordered an auto, that was my fate

But as for the job itself back then
Nothing changed, there was no Mother Hen
Which suited me right down to the ground
So telling work, was good for me, I found

Walking Figures, acrylic and charcoal on panel, 2009

I Am Still Me

I don't wear make-up any more
Or heels 3 inches to the floor
Contact lenses I can't put in
And I can no longer stay slim

But I'm still feminine you'll see
Despite this thing that's called PD
It will not get the better of me
This dreadful thing that's called PD

Nail polish goes here and there
And as for putting on underwear
Doing up clasps and putting in earrings
We just take for granted these things

But I'm still feminine you'll see
Despite this thing that's called PD
For inside I am still me
In spite of this, I'm still Becky

The Quake

A little twitch
A violent shake
Then stillness reigns
After the quake

Just a State of Mind

I used to think that Parkinson's was just a state of mind
But when I was diagnosed I left that thought behind
How can it be so different from one day to the next
This little thought bothered me, even had me quite perplexed

How is it that on one day I can walk perfectly well
Yet on other days the slightest little movement can be hell
Try telling someone without PD and I'm sure that you will find
That they will look right back at you thinking "It's just a state of mind!"

Walking Figure, oil on panel, 2009

What is Life All About?

"What is life all about?" I once heard someone say
It takes a lifetime to work out, and that's the price we pay
To go through life with nothing wrong really is a blessing
But for most of us that's not the case, God has his way of messing

We hope and pray that we are one of the lucky few
But to be given the blessed Parkinson's simply just won't do
Because for this condition, in present time there is no cure
So is this a challenge we cannot win, if so, bring it to the fore

On and Off Again

There are some days when I think I'm cool
no stiffness, nor shaking, not slow, there's no drool
on days like this when I feel a bit high
I wonder what some people think of this guy

"Why's he not using a stick" they may think
"he could eat without spilling his food or his drink.
He's standing there with a smile on his face
but he always looks blank in the workplace"

I could do with a meter alongside my head
and when I was drugged up, maybe it would be read
and as levels drop down and symptoms increase
the needle would move and display my disease

Iceberg

Standing leaning on my stick
people thinking I'm just fine
for coping with, whatever it is I am
coping with (I don't wear a sign)

Then pointlessly a limb begins to shake
people quickly stepping back
I look like I am in a quake
I know what they're thinking –
"What is the craic?"

Well let me tell you now
That the shake that you see
is only 10%
of the shake that's in me
which as well as a limb, shakes
my sense of myself,
my confidence
the way I feel about my ability
to do my job
to be a husband, father, friend
to take on something new

and in the end I find I bend to its will
and the worst I can do is to wish it ill
Because, you may know, this thing won't let go
once it's got you, it's got you for good

Passerby, acrylic on panel, 2009

Impact

Music used to matter
She played piano in big shows
Then one day PD came for her
And made her left arm slow

He played guitar, finger picking
His blues were mean and cold
Then one day PD came his way
And made his fingers old

The ivories she'd tickle
The strings that he would bend
The music they would play for joy
PD brought to an end

Chapter 3

Further on Down the Road

My Feet

I learnt to walk when I was one
Back then it was so much fun
And now it pains me to admit
Most of the time I have to sit

'Cos when I step I often stumble
oh shit, bollocks you hear me mumble
For my feet can't keep up with me
which is devastating when you need a pee

Left, right and right once more
I shuffle before I hit the floor
they try to trip me all the day
they just won't let me have my way

So I could have them amputated
and in a wheelchair be creative
I could act the fool, like a clown
without my feet bringing me down

It's My Brain

It's not my body it's my brain
That's driving me so insane
My body does whatever its told
My brain is becoming ever so bold

It tells one thing to do this, another to do that
Sometimes I look a proper prat
I look drunk when I've had none
To the point where people think "she's gone"

And at work some people think
I've got a problem with the drink
And if I'm honest I do, I can't stop
From stumbling and spilling every last drop

It's my broken brain that makes me roll
Around like I'm out of control
Writhing like a demented windmill
Before I get to take another pill

Which feeds my brain just what it needs
No, not nutrients and seeds
But drugs, chemicals are what I mean
More of that special Dopamine

One more thing before it's too late
Before my brain degenerates
Just one more thing I'd like for sure
Is a sodding Parkinson's cure!

My Legs

Off I go to take a walk
I've done it lots before
I concentrate and focus my gait
sure I can do it once more.

But my legs they start to falter
my pace I find I have to alter
my legs turn to lead, something's gone wrong
my breathing is heavy, but I've not been gone long…

…and my sense of me falls right out of the tree.

Study for *Walking Figure,* charcoal on paper, 2009

Reality

Tremors – not a film, a reality
Shakes – not a drink, a reality
Stiffness – not temporary, a reality
Slow – not a game, a reality

and reality for me is what you cannot see
the fear and the anxiety
the tears I cry regularly
and all because of this PD

I Wonder

I wonder what you think of me
Yes, you over there, yes, I can see
I'm sure you think I've had a drink
For sure… yes you do

I don't care what you think of me
I am bigger than you, you see
I know I haven't had a drop
so I don't care… yes I do

Why do I let it bother me?
That you're taking the 'Mickey'
I move away pretty quickly
For a 'Parky'… yes I do

I walk tall when I enter a room
I'm proud when I'm out and about
and then I stagger and stumble and fumble
and wonder if you found me out – yes I do

Options

I don't know where my street cred's gone
I used to know the score,
But now each day I wrack my mind
to find something to say

I'm not the man I used to be
confident and strong
now I seem to worry about
everything all day long

Where has he gone that man I was
he's gone, I've lost my voice
I cannot live the life I knew
I can't go on like I had choice

Walking Man: After Muybridge, monoprint on paper, 2009

Frozen

Frozen in time, frozen in space
Frozen body, frozen face
Pop a pill
What a thrill
Movement at last
But it soon goes past
Frozen in time, frozen in space
Frozen body, frozen face

Desperandum

When we first met, I had no idea how you would affect me
How intimate we would become
How deep our interdependence would be.
I did not recognise the part you would play in my life's journey
I did not know how you would entrance me by getting inside my head
How you would seduce my libido, leaving me flopping, rudderless in my manhood.
How you would slowly…
So slowly…
Take me over – lock, stock and barrel!

And then you convert to a bunny boiler!
I want to go, you say "oh no, no, no"
I start to walk away – I say walk I mean stagger
"Get off my legs," I yell at you,
"They're mine," you call as you swagger away
and then return and start flapping my arms.

Like a lover in a hotel room, Parkinson's absorbs you completely
But as you start to learn more about the dirty tricks
and start to cool off from this mad affair
Realisation dawns that you will be found out
and you'll live with the cursed thing, forever.

I'm Fine

"How do you feel today?"
"I'm fine"
Ask me again tomorrow and I'll say
"I'm fine"

No one wants to hear you're not
I'd rather it were something you forgot

So how do I feel today?
"I'm fine!"

Dancer in Rehearsal, acrylic on canvas, 2004

Reality Check

sometimes there are lighter moments in any condition,
so when they appear let's embrace them
not treat them with suspicion
they surely pop-up for a reason
which can't be to wither and die
so let's do our best to meet their "request"
and reward them with laughter and smiles.

If something is funny it's funny
and laughing at it isn't a joke
and if other people whine
the problem is theirs not mine.
Laughing at something amusing
doesn't mean you're giving a diss
it just means that something's amusing
it's not like watching a briss.

So leave me to my laughter, or better yet join in
if we laugh at trials together, who knows we may yet win
so gather as many as possible, let's all give it a spin
when something is funny it's funny and I'm not about to give in.

Chapter 4

Family and Friends

My Friend with PD
A Friend's Perspective

I have a friend who has PD
She shakes and is real wobbly
We used to go to watch race cars
But now we sit and count the stars

Our walking days have come to an end
They are too difficult for my friend
Our holidays are more rest than play
'Cos she gets tired in the day

It's hard to watch her degenerate
To understand her mental state
To see her struggle with her clothes
Its hard some days to blow her nose

Our time together has changed somewhat
And our friendship has gone through a lot
But she is still a good friend to me
Despite the diagnosis of PD

Telling You

Telling you was hard for me
I felt ashamed and guilty
I had something only old people get
I was 29 let's not forget

But you accepted what I had to say
You didn't want to though on that day
The tone was serious and sad
But this was me, it couldn't be all bad

I'd had all the test, scans and an x-ray
and with certainty you'd hear me say
that there was one thing I knew for sure
at least it wasn't a brain tumour

Kid's Talk

How do you tell a child you're ill
and the reason you take that special pill
Would they understand your plight
That, against which you fight
Do you put it in baby talk
About the fact that you can't walk
But that it only happens on some days
And it's at this point their eyes glaze
"Mummy can I have a lolly please?"

On the Threshold, acrylic on panel, 2009

Wedding Day

I'm speaking at Richard's wedding
it will be such a lovely day
the only problem and the thing I'm dreading
is that I don't know what to say

I'm a very proud dad there's no doubt about that
and a skilled public speaker to boot
I've spoken on topics 'bout both life and the law
but for Richard and Jen I just don't know the score

This damned PD is crippling me
and stopping me doing my best
I'll have to establish a lower benchmark
for the new me to measure instead

But I'm speaking at Richard's wedding
to welcome his lovely Jen,
There's a welcome for both her and hers,
I know, I'll say something in verse

Telling Mum

"Fancy some lunch?"
Of course you do
Your child is so grown up
He can take you for lunch, pay the bill without a flinch
But he's always a child to you

"I have some news," I venture over coffee
"I'm not as well as you might wish.
I've seen a doctor or 3 or 4
For quite a while they were not sure
But now it seems I have Parkinson's…"

The silence falls and hits the ground
You look quite blank and stare around
The words I have spoken take their toll
As you try to make sense of my tale

'That can't be right' I see you think
'He can't be ill with Parkinson's'
I don't know what to say to him
"They must have got it wrong."

Overleaf: *My Mother Walking the Old House 1,* acrylic on panel, 2008

Chapter 5

Looking Ahead

Rhythm of Reality

Sticky feet set up a rhythm
That neither scans nor rhymes
The whole of me needs attention
I act kinda tough, but you're not blind

Walking, talking, dancing, singing
Is who we all used to be
Shaking, quaking, stop-go driving
are the people you now see

Family sitting on a settee
Take some things for granted
Are you all sitting comfortably?
Wriggle, jiggle, oops, need a pee

Rhythm is the heartbeat of life
and it feels much better
when it's slow and steady
and to face the world, you are ready.

PD strips your steadiness
It leaves you less than prep'd
To face the wall, or anything at all.

Why Not Me?

Why is this me?
I'm supposed to ask
I really can't be bothered
It is what it is and I am what I am
Which is all that one could wish

Truth be told this new me is quite an amusing chap
he fumbles and dithers and… actually it's crap
to be like this:
> too tired to work
> too drugged to think
> too forgetful to remember
> too scared to speak.

> It's a curse, not a blessing
> And it's not that funny either

Just Like a Junkie

Sweating torrents as drugs foment
pathetic brain cells to dispense
their last microns of dopamine
to smooth the way through my day

Not a gentle sheen, not a ladies light touch
but a full on, full-scale manly flush
soaking through my shirt
It could shift ground in dirt

"It's caused by drugs," I'm told each time
I ask for reason to go with the rhyme
they're switching on or switching off
they can't help the sweating and now I'm just betting
they don't know why or the wherefore
and sweating's just one more small thing

But for me it has the discomfort, the embarrassment of facing my peers
with a shirt stained with soaking wet patches and a jacket that is also smeared
with water pouring from my head and my hair's now plastered to it
so it's not just one more small thing or a slight exaggeration of life
it's an affront to my self-image, an affront to my wife
an unacceptable part of a Parkinson's life.

My Mother Walking the Old House 2, acrylic on panel, 2008

The Future?

What does the future hold for people just like me?
You're like me if you have this thing called PD
I once said to a journalist "it's not Parkinson's, it's mine"
And the press, they picked up on it, so maybe it's a sign
That times they are a changing and the fight maybe we'll win
But frankly "a cure within five years" is wearing a bit thin
What are the drug companies doing to combat this sad plight?
And do we think that it's enough to wage a war, to fight
I'd like to think we have the backing of each and every one
But if we did then surely this battle we'd already have won
So I take it upon myself to drive the message to
The individuals researching that cure for both me and you.

Covered in Wee?

Oh what does life have in store for me?
Sat in a Nursing Home covered in wee?
Or will I be home being a Mother, a Wife?
Oh I wish I knew what PD had in store for my life!

The days with PD are unpredictable, they vary
Which is sometimes good, but more often scary
On good days I walk with only a limp
On bad days I shuffle and drift like a blimp

But it's the little things that non PDers don't know
Like chewing, talking loud enough, being able to swallow
Like losing more confidence day after day
Because all that you hear is "what's that you say?"

I hate looking drunk when I've not touched a drop
And stumbling so fast, not able to stop
Being so very tired but not able to sleep
And the slightest little thing making me weep

The drugs help my movement but change my persona
I was never really a whiner, a whinger or moaner
But this year I promised myself would be great!
Because in April, it's the ball, Illuminate!

I have the opportunity to change people's lives
Raising money so PDers like me can stay home as Husbands or Wives
I know now there will be no Nursing Home for me
'Cos I don't fancy being covered in wee!

Drooling

Saliva seeps slowly
through the slackened seal
of the right side of my mouth.
It gathers in my beard,
as if held by a JML Magic Mop
until it reaches critical mass
and then it drips,
slowly so slowly,
onto whatever is below.

My saliva drops are very 'right on'
They absolutely do not discriminate,
They will drip on anyone,
regardless of circumstances,
race, creed, colour or sex
regardless of me,
of my feelings,
of injury to my sense of self.

This is how, given time
A young onset Parky Person gets a face made of wet stone.
We're not really old, we just have a blankness of expression
Oh… and a slack seal at the side of our mouths

My Mother Walking the Old House 3, acrylic on panel, 2008

Science has Its Part to Play

It screws with your legs and your arms and your mind
This unwelcome squatter, this visitor of mine
It might make you stiff or too slow or confused
And whatever you do, you know you will lose

And then there's the drugs, they do for you too
Make you feel sick or drowsy, just lousy
They're good for you one way
Heads or tails and you lose

In science's eyes, there is fascination
"What does that drug do"?, "What, you can't have a poo?"
"That doesn't sound right," they don't mean to be trite
But my reality is their story too

And as you get older it's less of a issue
People talk over your head
"Does he take sugar?" is the standard error
And from there its downhill and to bed.

So when in your dotage and pissing yourself
Remember the scientists helped out
They developed a wee pad that's easy to change
And the cup with the lid and a spout.

Chapter 6

You've Got
To Laugh

or else you'd cry

Patience?

They want to know what patients want
so they ask the least patient of all, (that's Becky)
who knows exactly what patients want
which is not to be patients

Shaking Can Be Useful
If You Let It Be

Shaking can be useful if you let it be
I could make a cocktail for you and me
See, not all things are so bad with PD,
'Cos shaking can be useful if you let it be

Try airing out your clothes by holding them, you'll see
It gets the creases out almost instantly
A little shake here and there, with a one, two, three
I told you shaking can be useful if you let it be

See, you have to look upon it very positively
Try finding situations where shaking is the key
I can think of one almost immediately
Where shaking can be useful if you let it be

Limerick

there was a young woman from Worcester
whose soubriquet in those days was Beckster
she wanted a ball to illuminate all
so she had one and got 3 million pennies

My Mother Walking the Old House 4, acrylic on panel, 2008

Haiku

Haiku has a rule
seven syls on second line
otherwise do five

Shaking stiff and scared
refusing to play P's game
looking disabled

Feet sticking, body falls
just how PD wants it to
break an arm and cry

Lying, lying often
sometimes sleeping, sometimes not
not liking yourself

Living, loving life
Long days become filled with strife
loving hating life

Visible signs easy
inner damage not so clear
so no-one sees it

My Mother: Against the Light, acrylic on panel, 2007

Research can be Slightly Shocking!

There's lots of research going on with big words to describe it
but the one I want to comment on well, I've never seen anything like it
my head was wrapped in a surgeons cap, a grid inscribed upon it
a magnetic field was then discharged just centimetres from it.

There were two striking feelings that went with this discharge;
one is helpless jumping hands, the other much more harsh
it's rather like someone's flicking your skull; it was somewhat unexpected
this is research into swallowing, and PWPs who are so affected.

I swallowed a tube of electronic gizmos, but only half way down
it had to hang there down my throat, it often made me frown
I swallowed many spoonfuls of tasty barium
while the video x-ray showed it dropping to my tum.

I had to blow through empty tubes and suck upon some plastic
and finally I had to snort (from my nose) something elastic.
I couldn't have a cup of tea, not coffee or a piece of toast
but apart from that I was treated as the man who was the most
important person there that day; I know I had my part to play
I'm not saying I've done my bit, but I wasn't put off by a little hit.

Chapter 7

Nil Desperandum

The Winds of Change

The Winds of Change how they now blow
Despite the fact that I'm still slow
I see a much rosier view ahead
I won't be banished to my bed
For I have changed my view on things
I look forward to the challenges life brings
And no, not those caused by PD
But those that have been generated by me
I'll work for as long as I possibly can
So long as I can contribute man for man
And when the time comes to pack it in
It will be the close of one Chapter with another to begin

For As Long As I Can

For as long as I can
I will be the person I always wanted to be
For as long as I can
I promise that you will have the best of me
For as long as I can
I will hold your hand and walk with you in the sun
For as long as I can
I will make sure that every day we have lots of fun
And when the day comes that I can no longer
do these things above
Remember that you will always be here
in my heart my love

PD?

PMA, that's what they say – A positive mental attitude
"They" always talk in acronyms – which sometimes look quite rude
PMA or PMT it's just one letter changed
Where things could go from positive to something else, deranged

And who are "they" anyway – the ones of whom we speak
The ones who make up the shortened words and try to be unique

There's NI, VAT and PAYE if you're talking about money
There's LOL and PMSL if you're trying to be funny
There's CO_2 and H_2O if we're talking scientific
There's REF: and XXX if you want to be specific

But the one that I see most these days but now don't give a damn
Is the one that describes the condition I have and not the person I am

Figure in Movement, monoprint, 2009

My Parkie Friends

We belong to a unique club my Parkie friends and I
We all have something in common, on each we rely

We understand what it is that's going on behind the scenes
We recognise it in the eyes and see the inward screams

We know what goes on with the drugs, we don't need to spell it out
Voices do not need to be heard, for we hear each other shout

It's like we are all soul mates who are all in the same gang
But occasionally one goes pop, whilst another one goes bang

We are all in this together but alone we sometimes feel
For behind closed doors it is just us and the PD is so real

So out of ourselves we must aim to be, a member of a team
All for one and one for all, to march together it would seem

Would be the sensible thing to do, as many heads are better than one
And without our group of Parkie friends how can the battle be won?

Falling Down

It's easy to fall flat on your face
a whole lot harder to get up
you could lie there for good,
whilst doubting if you should
adopt such a passive position
but it's so very easy to let the whole thing overwhelm you
to lie there and roll with it
to look round helplessly for assistance
to want to be cared for and looked after and dependent.

It's kind of hard to get up
and kick over the traces
and say I'm not giving up
and I recognise the faces
of those who deny me
my independence, my freedom,
myself.

Dawn

Down
Face down
In the battlefield's mud
That skirmish lost, that battle too
The war yet to be won

Defeated
I lie for now defeated
I rest and weep and mourn my loss
And then, tears depleted, slowly
I lift my head

Dawn
A new dawn
Lights my face and warms the land
After thought, Hope is raised,
Never dashed for long

Waking Figure, acrylic on panel, 2009

Today

Dawn broke
its racket shattering my superficial sleep
I lie still, eyes shut
and wonder how to face today

A warm smile "I'm fine today"
to any who might enquire
no point in going into detail
no point in causing woe.

Sit on my hands
tension in my leg
cover the tremor
wish it were dead

well one day maybe
a cure, its not crazy to
think about,
it won't be pulled from a hat

But with funding and research
and a push from the crowd
someone is bound to find the key
and open our locks and set us free

Embattled

The Warrior settled his mount again
the Warrior raised his lance again
the Warrior drew his sword again
and into battle rode again

The enemy appeared again
ready to hit and spit again
wanting to do harm again
hungry for his prey again

The Warrior breathed a sigh again
he rubbed his weary eye again
he sighted toward his prey again
and rode into the fray again

The enemy was everywhere again
muscles undermined again
movement in decline again
a comprehensive maul again

The Lance hit home, spot-on again
the wound at once it healed again
his sword hit true again
and blood it drew again

The enemy licked its wounds again
and to full strength it grew again
the damage it would do again
it already knew again

The Warrior settled his mount again
the Warrior raised his lance again
the Warrior drew his sword again
and into battle rode again

Hoping

"What's the point?" I hear
"it's going to happen anyway"
despondency, gloom, settling around
like a mist creeping from the swamp

"It is as likely to be as not to be" I say
"it may not happen anyway"
reality check blows mist
like the morning sun burns it away

"They're nowhere near" I hear
"there's not a chance they'll do it"
Despair, like rain in the air
invisible but real and soaking

"You don't know that" I say
"they might crack it tomorrow"
Hope, like love, springs eternal
the Sun lifts over the horizon

And so I argue back and forth
Doubt tempered by Hope
waiting to hear that a cure is near
waiting to see what might be.

Young Boy Walking, acrylic on panel, 2009

Hunting

Parkinson's Disease is a bastard
it scratches and bites
it goes where it likes
it's resistant to all known traps
so it's time that we built a new one,
Made it so very failsafe
that it won't only trap and contain it
it will stop it from causing more strife

It will no longer have free passage
no more will it ruin our lives
the club will be closed, the doors firmly locked
new members will not be exposed
to the tyranny of drugs
to the fear of the knife
to the consequential doings
of a Parkinson life

Figure Turning, watercolour on paper, 2009

P.M.A. (Positive Mental Attitude)

I have PD it does not have me
I see my life more positively
I live each day as if it were my last
As time goes by so very fast
My glass is now always half full
I have a PMA, no bull
There is no need to be glum
I have everything I need, and then some

The 'Blessing' that is PD

One might argue, one might disagree
About the 'blessing' that is PD
Each one of us has our own degree
Of what we call truth or insanity

On one hand one might say it's a curse
Or use profanity which can be terse
But used in such a lively verse
Makes it sound much less worse

On the other hand it could change you for the good
Make you consider things you never would
Give you the confidence to feel you could
Make you do the things you should

PD is life changing not something from which you die
Without it could I honestly say would I be 'happier', no not I
For because of it my aspiration is to 'reach for the sky'
And with it my desire is to try, try and try

So, is PD a blessing? For me I'd say who knows
But at least my life has a purpose not to dwell on the woes
I like a challenge although I wouldn't say "anything goes"
It's a personal battle and I'm in the throes…

The End

And so we come to the end of our time
these poems with no structure
some don't even rhyme
each one is heartfelt
and based upon fact
but if they still don't do it for you
the pictures will have impact.

Words of Wisdom

Life is what you make it. Whilst Parkinson's Disease may take away your ability to do certain things, it also can enrich your life making you see things differently. So, seize life and treat each day as if it were your last. I know I do.

— Becky Hurd, 2010

Personal experience drew me to the subject of walking: from charting the first hesitant steps of my children, to watching the determination and courage of my mother refusing to accept the debilitating progress of Parkinson's disease. Recently I have worked in the University of Salford's Podiatry Department which has increased my wonder at the extraordinary choreographies of walking. The simple act of putting one foot in front of the other – so natural it seems for most of us, so hard-won for others.

— Ghislaine Howard, 2011

When Life Gives you Lemons, make Lemonade!

It could be worse.

— Ray Wegrzyn, both too often to record